Original title:
Through the Pain

Copyright © 2024 Swan Charm
All rights reserved.

Author: Kene Elistrand
ISBN HARDBACK: 978-9916-79-239-1
ISBN PAPERBACK: 978-9916-79-240-7
ISBN EBOOK: 978-9916-79-241-4

Sacred Tears

In the stillness of the night, grace falls,
Each tear a prayer, echoing the calls.
The souls that weep are blessed in their plight,
For from their sorrow, blooms eternal light.

Heaven's gaze upon the broken heart,
A tapestry of love, where we each play a part.
Every drop an offering, every sigh a plea,
In the garden of faith, we find our tree.

The Path of Sacrifice

Walk we the road where shadows convene,
Bearing the burden, unseen but keen.
With each step forward, the heart expands,
In the light of surrender, we join sacred hands.

Courage is found in the whisper of pain,
In the silence of giving, we break every chain.
To offer our lives for the greater good,
Is to walk in the footsteps where the Savior stood.

Divine Comfort in Despair

In the valley deep, where hope seems lost,
Echoes of mercy remind us of cost.
The gentle hand wipes the tears from our face,
In the shadow of grief, we discover His grace.

Through the struggles and trials, we come to see,
That in moments of doubt, we are set free.
For every burden carried, a blessing grows,
And in the depths of sorrow, true love bestows.

Whispers of Redemption

In the evening hush, we hear the call,
Soft whispers of grace, enveloping all.
Each heart that falters finds a way back home,
In the tapestry woven, together we roam.

The light of forgiveness shines bright and clear,
Revealing the beauty that lies within fear.
In the stillness of night, hope is reborn,
And the whispers of love usher in the dawn.

The Cross We Bear

Upon our shoulders, burdens rest,
In trials deep, we seek the blessed.
With faith as light, we walk the road,
Together we share this heavy load.

Through thorns and stones, our spirits rise,
In darkest nights, love never lies.
We forge our path with steadfast grace,
In every wound, we find His face.

Though shadows loom, we stand as one,
With hearts ablaze beneath the sun.
The cross we bear, a sacred gift,
In pain and joy, our souls uplift.

Echoes of the Silent Cry

In the quiet night, a soul does weep,
Beneath the stars, secrets deep.
A whisper lost in winds of fate,
Yearning hearts, we ache and wait.

For every prayer that's fallen still,
There lies a strength within our will.
Through silent cries, His voice we find,
In shadows dark, our hopes entwined.

With every tear that stains the ground,
A testament to love unbound.
In sorrow's depth, we rise anew,
With echoes rich, His promise true.

A Soul's Voyage Through Tempest

O'er rolling waves, the spirit sails,
Through stormy nights and whispered gales.
Each crest a test, each trough a prayer,
Guided by faith, we journey there.

With every thunder, courage grows,
In darkest trials, His love bestows.
The compass points to shores unknown,
Through raging seas, our seeds are sown.

A lighthouse shines in the heart's domain,
Through trials faced, no loss, no gain.
With sails unfurled, we seek the light,
In skies of gray, our dreams take flight.

The Prayer of the Forsaken

In solitude, we raise our plea,
To skies above, our spirits free.
With trembling hands and hopes laid bare,
We seek the wisdom found in care.

Though shadows cast their chilling grip,
We find our strength in love's sweet sip.
For in the silence, whispers bloom,
A promise held against the gloom.

So hear our hearts, O Divine grace,
In every sorrow, find our place.
The prayer of those who seem alone,
A bond unbroken, faith our stone.

The Embrace of the Unseen

In stillness, whispers breathe,
The unseen guides our way.
With every step, we believe,
Hope and love in the sway.

From shadows, light will emerge,
In hearts that seek the Divine.
With faith, our souls will surge,
Transcending the earthly line.

In silence, we find the song,
Echoes of grace above.
Together, we all belong,
Wrapped in the arms of love.

Though trials may darken the nights,
Our spirits shall not bend.
For in the depths, purest sights,
Reveal the faithful blend.

In unity, we rise as one,
In faith, our journey grows.
For every battle fought and won,
The unseen love bestows.

Broken Vessels, Sacred Crowns

In cracks, true beauty lies,
Imperfect made divine.
Each scar a tale that flies,
A heart with purpose, you find.

The weight of burdens shared,
Makes us stronger in our plight.
In brokenness, we're paired,
With grace that shines so bright.

Each vessel holds a story,
A journey through the fire.
In ashes, we find glory,
As love ignites the desire.

With every tear that's shed,
We gather courage anew.
Where darkness almost led,
The dawn breaks fresh and true.

Together, we wear crowns,
Of trials, joy, and pain.
In life's chaotic towns,
We rise and shine again.

Grace in the Abyss

In depths of quiet sorrow,
Where shadows cast their nets.
A glimmer greets tomorrow,
With love that never forgets.

The weight of night is heavy,
Yet faith ignites a flame.
In chaos, hearts are steady,
Transformed, we rise with name.

Each struggle, a testament,
To grace that gently flows.
In trials, He is present,
Through loss, His presence grows.

Though storms may tear asunder,
And fears loom like the sea,
Within the heart, a thunder,
Of peace that sets us free.

In the abyss, we discover,
The depth of love profound.
As shadows cease to hover,
In grace, our hope is found.

A Covenant with Discomfort

In discomfort, we are chosen,
To walk the narrow line.
For every heart that's broken,
A purpose to define.

With every trial we face,
A lesson here to learn.
In struggle, we find grace,
That helps our spirits turn.

The path may seem unyielding,
Yet strength is found in prayer.
Through every wound, we're healing,
As hope becomes our air.

In fires that cleanse the soul,
We rise with every fall.
In weakness, we are whole,
Embraced in love's sweet call.

Thus, with each step we take,
A promise forged in pain.
With faith, we will awake,
In discomfort, light shall reign.

The Voyage of the Brokenhearted

In the depths where shadows dwell,
Whispers of hearts begin to swell.
Each tear a testament of pain,
A journey carved through silent rain.

With every sorrow, a spark ignites,
Guiding souls through darkest nights.
In the distance, hope's faint glow,
A promise whispered soft and low.

They sail on waves of lost embrace,
Searching for a sacred space.
Through the trials, they rise and learn,
For broken hearts, in love, will burn.

As dawn breaks o'er the restless sea,
Wounds uncovered long to be free.
A vessel forged by faith's pure light,
Guided by the radiant night.

In the midst of sorrow's storm,
Hearts unite, a unity warm.
Bearing burdens hand in hand,
Together, they shall bravely stand.

Tapestry of Trials

Threads of life woven with care,
Each strand a burden we bear.
In shadows deep, we find our grace,
A tapestry of the human race.

Through trials fierce, our spirits rise,
Reflecting truth in broken ties.
Every knot a story told,
In the struggle, the heart grows bold.

From sorrow's loom, peace is spun,
Each battle fought, a victory won.
Through every tear that stains the cloth,
Emerges light, a sacred oath.

And though the fibers may fray,
In unity, they find their way.
Embracing scars, they intertwine,
A sacred bond, pure and divine.

In the patterns fierce and wild,
Resilience blooms, the spirit's child.
A tapestry rich in love embraced,
In trials faced, the heart finds grace.

The Opulence of Suffering

In valleys low where shadows creep,
The heart, it learns the depth of weep.
Yet in the ache, a treasure lies,
A strength unveiled, a spirit wise.

With every wound, the soul expands,
Eclipsing fear with open hands.
In suffering's grasp, we uncover gold,
A wisdom vast, a truth retold.

Through trials faced, we rise anew,
In darkest nights, the stars break through.
Opulence found in brokenness,
A blessing born from earth's duress.

In the crucible of aching heart,
Beauty blooms, a sacred art.
The opulence of suffering dear,
Reveals the path we hold most near.

With every trial, we learn to dance,
In pain, there lies a sacred chance.
Embracing hurt, we find our song,
A symphony of love made strong.

Embracing the Inferno

In twilight's grasp, the flames arise,
An inferno ignites the skies.
With hearts aflame, we walk the path,
Embracing trials, facing wrath.

Through fire's heat, the spirit's born,
From ashes, hope is gently worn.
Each blaze a lesson, fierce and bright,
Illuminating darkest night.

With open arms, we take the flame,
Transforming pain to love's sweet name.
In every trial, hearts are forged,
In the inferno, faith enlarged.

The heat may rise, the shadows loom,
Yet in the darkness, we find room.
To dance within the sacred fire,
Awakening the soul's desire.

Embracing chaos, we start to see,
In the inferno, we find our plea.
Through every spark, a truth conveyed,
In flames of love, our fears allayed.

Beneath the Veil of Tears

Beneath the veil of gentle tears,
We seek the light that softly nears.
In shadowed heart, our sorrows dwell,
Yet in our grief, we hear the bell.

The whispers rise, a sacred song,
To lift the weary, weak, and strong.
With every drop, a prayer we send,
Transforming pain to hope, our friend.

A tapestry of wounds now sewn,
The fabric of our faith has grown.
In every loss, His love abounds,
In every ache, His mercy sounds.

Through every trial, we find His grace,
In every tear, we seek His face.
Beneath the veil, we heal, we mend,
In Christ, our journey has no end.

The Prayer of the Pilgrim

In distant lands, the pilgrim roams,
With weary heart and dreams of homes.
Each step a prayer, each breath a plea,
To find the path that sets him free.

The road is long, the night is cold,
In search of truth more precious than gold.
With every mile, surrender made,
In faith, the burdens start to fade.

A whispered prayer in shadows deep,
His promises, the soul will keep.
For in the trials we endure,
Our spirit's strength, forever pure.

As dawn breaks forth, the light reveals,
The grace that flows, the love that heals.
With open heart, our journey's end,
In every footstep, He'll descend.

From Desolation to Divinity

From desolation, hearts arise,
In silent prayers beneath the skies.
Through darkest valleys, shadows creep,
Yet in our souls, the hope we keep.

Each tear a seed, from grief it grows,
In barren lands, the spirit glows.
With every ache, we're being forged,
In trials thick, our faith enlarged.

In desolation, grace we find,
The gentle touch, the loving kind.
For every storm that raged within,
Brings forth the light, the joy, the hymn.

The path from pain to peace is sure,
With faith in Him, our hearts endure.
From dust to divinity, we rise,
In every breath, our spirit flies.

An Offering of Brokenness

An offering of brokenness we bear,
With open hands, we lift our prayer.
In vulnerability, our souls laid bare,
Through every crack, we find Him there.

The shattered pieces, scattered wide,
In His embrace, we choose to hide.
Each wound a story, every scar,
In depths of sorrow, we find our star.

From ashes rise a fragrant grace,
In brokenness, we seek His face.
With hearts unguarded, truth takes flight,
In surrender, darkness turns to light.

An offering, a sweet refrain,
In every loss, in every pain.
We bring our hearts, though bent and torn,
In Christ, anew, we are reborn.

In the Hands of Hope

In the stillness of night, we pray,
With hearts that yearn for the light.
Guided by faith's gentle sway,
Embracing dreams within our sight.

Each whisper carries a sacred sound,
Echoes of love from above.
With every promise, we are found,
In the arms of hope, we move.

The burdens of worry, we release,
As grace envelops our way.
In surrender, find our peace,
Trusting in tomorrow's day.

Together we rise, hand in hand,
With spirits ignited and bold.
In the promise of faith, we stand,
As the stories of our hearts unfold.

In the hands of hope, we abide,
With courage that never sways.
Through valleys low, and mountains wide,
Our souls are lifted in praise.

Tears as Sacred Waters

In the depths of sorrow, we find,
Tears like rivers, flowing free.
Each drop a gift for the divine,
Cleansing souls, bringing us to be.

Sacred waters, healing wounds,
In grief, we gather strength anew.
For every heart that gently swoons,
Love blooms like flowers in dew.

When shadows fall, and hope seems lost,
Remember, tears can bring light.
In the breaking, there is cost,
Yet faith will guide us through the night.

Let the waters cleanse your spirit,
Wash away doubts that remain.
In every tear, a lesson in it,
Finding joy amidst the pain.

So we honor each sacred tear,
For they remind us we are whole.
In the embrace of love, we steer,
Our journey deepens, blesses the soul.

The Path of Hidden Blessings

In wanderings deep, we may stray,
Yet blessings are hidden from view.
With faith as our guide, we will stay,
To discover the wonders that are true.

Through trials that shape, bend and break,
Each moment, a step on this road.
In the choices we make, we awake,
Finding grace in the heavy load.

Glimmers of hope in the darkest night,
Reminders that love always reigns.
In the challenges faced, we ignite,
A strength that overcomes the chains.

As we walk, hand in hand with grace,
We cherish the lessons bestowed.
With each hidden blessing we trace,
Our spirits grow, boldly bestowed.

So let us embrace this sacred way,
With gratitude woven in heart.
Through the path of blessings, we pray,
Together we are never apart.

A Hymn for the Haunted

In the silence where shadows creep,
Voices echo of sorrow and pain.
Yet within the heart, hope cannot sleep,
As the spirit rises, breaking the chain.

A hymn for the haunted, we sing,
To soothe the souls lost in the night.
In the darkest, let love take wing,
Shining bright, a beacon of light.

From the depths of despair, we call,
Gathering strength in unity's grace.
Together we rise, never to fall,
Embracing the warmth in this space.

Let the echoes of past gently fade,
As the dawn breaks, bringing new air.
In forgiveness, our hearts are laid,
A promise that love is always there.

So we hold hands, the haunted and free,
In a chorus where all hearts unite.
Through the struggles, we claim victory,
In the hymn of our shared, sacred light.

Journey of the Broken

In valleys low, the lost ones tread,
With weary hearts and dreams now fled.
Yet in the darkness, a spark ignites,
A whispered prayer in lonely nights.

With every step, they find the way,
Through shattered hopes that still betray.
But grace surrounds, like morning dew,
Restoring faith to hearts anew.

O weary soul, take heart and rise,
For every tear, the Savior cries.
The journey long, yet love prevails,
Through storms and trials, peace regales.

In brokenness, a path unfolds,
Where dreams once splintered turn to gold.
With every scar, a story told,
Of faith renewed and hope retold.

So walk with courage, through the pain,
For in the loss, there's much to gain.
The journey crafted with divine care,
Will lead us home, forever fair.

When the Soul Laments

In silence deep, the spirit cries,
As shadows linger, hope defies.
A heart laid bare, in grief it moans,
For mercy's touch, the weary groans.

The midnight hour holds no reprieve,
Yet in the darkness, we believe.
A flicker shines in sorrow's pall,
A promise whispered, 'You will not fall.'

When dreams are lost, in bitter night,
We seek the dawn, the guiding light.
In every ache, the lesson sown,
A strength unseen, now brightly grown.

O heart that weeps, do not despair,
For grace abounds, in every prayer.
As seasons change, the spirit mends,
And in the storm, the soul ascends.

The lament turns to songs of praise,
As hope awakens through the haze.
In every tear, a seed is sown,
To bloom anew, in love we've known.

In the Company of Shadows

In twilight soft, the shadows play,
A haunting dance at end of day.
Yet in their midst, a light appears,
To calm the heart, dispel the fears.

For every shadow that must roam,
A guiding star will lead us home.
In solace found, we learn to trust,
The gentle hand that carries us.

The trials faced, like rivers wide,
Can wash away the pain inside.
In company of shadows, we
Find hope and strength in unity.

The path is fraught with mystery,
Yet faith will guide our steps, you see.
For in the dark, a whisper calls,
In every heart, the spirit sprawls.

So walk with grace, through darkest night,
For shadows flee at dawn's first light.
In every wound, a lesson learned,
In every heart, a fire burned.

The Spirit's Resilient Call

From depths of sorrow, a voice will rise,
A tender pull towards the skies.
Through trials faced, the spirit's song,
Will guide us right, when all feels wrong.

In every storm, a promise stands,
The whispered truth of loving hands.
For in the heart of darkest night,
The spirit calls, to find the light.

With every breath, resilience grows,
In faith's embrace, our courage flows.
So rise above the fleeting pain,
For love endures, and hope will reign.

In valleys low and mountains high,
The spirit soars, it will not die.
Through every hardship, joy will walk,
In silence heard, the spirit's talk.

So heed the call, awaken now,
With every step, take faith's great vow.
For in the journey, love unfolds,
And every heart will find its gold.

The Strength in Surrender

In quiet faith, we lay our fears,
A gentle hand wipes away our tears.
Beneath the weight, our spirits rise,
In surrender's grace, our hope complies.

When burdens swell and shadows cast,
A whispered prayer brings light at last.
In brokenness, we find our peace,
From ashes cold, our hearts release.

Through trials steep, we walk the night,
With every step, we seek the light.
In trust divine, our souls align,
In surrender's arms, our love defined.

The strength we gain in letting go,
A faith profound, a deeper flow.
In softest moments, truth prevails,
As love's sweet song within us sails.

Together bound, we share the quest,
In humble hearts, we find our rest.
The strength we crave, in God's embrace,
In surrender's dance, we find our place.

Eden from the Ashes

From flames of sorrow, new blooms rise,
In darkest nights, a dawn complies.
The earth has wept, the skies have moaned,
Yet through the pain, our hearts have grown.

In shattered dreams, the seeds are sown,
In every loss, a blessing shown.
With faith ignited, we shall see,
From ashes deep, a new Eden be.

As rivers flow from mountain high,
So hope does spring, beneath the sky.
In trials faced, we find the grace,
Where love's embrace becomes our space.

We walk the path where shadows play,
Yet find a light to guide the way.
In every tear, a story told,
Of love reborn, of hearts turned gold.

Together we rise, hand in hand,
In unity, we bravely stand.
From ashes dark, a garden blooms,
In faith and love, our spirit looms.

Resurrecting the Spirit

In valleys low, our spirits sigh,
Yet from the depths, our wings will fly.
With hearts revived, we face the dawn,
In every loss, a strength reborn.

Through trials fierce, we learn to stand,
In every struggle, a guiding hand.
With faith as fuel, we cross the void,
In resurrecting, our hearts are buoyed.

The light within us starts to swell,
In whispered hope, the promise tells.
We rise again, though bruised and scarred,
In spirit's dance, our souls unmarred.

With every breath, we shed the past,
Through pain and loss, our love will last.
In trusting grace, we find our way,
Resurrected, we greet the day.

Together bound in sacred trust,
From every storm, we rise we must.
In spirit's flight, we glimpse the shield,
Of faith renewed, our hearts revealed.

Love's Labyrinth of Hurt

In corridors where shadows creep,
Our hearts entwined in secrets deep.
Through tangled paths of joy and pain,
We seek the light, a love's refrain.

In moments raw, when tears ensue,
Each broken piece brings forth the new.
Through hurtful times, we find our voice,
In love's embrace, we make our choice.

With every turn, the heart must learn,
To dance with fire, the passion burn.
In pain redoubled, the trust unwinds,
Yet hope remains, as love still binds.

In the labyrinth, we find our way,
Through trials fierce, love has its say.
In every corner, shadows play,
Yet brighter shines the break of day.

Together we rise, hand in hand,
In whispers soft, we understand.
Though hurt may shape the journey's art,
In love's embrace, we heal the heart.

Chains That Bind

In shadows deep, our hearts entangled,
We seek the light, but fear has wrangled.
Each whispered prayer, a fragile thread,
A vow of faith, where angels tread.

The burdens we carry, a sacred weight,
In trust we stand, at mercy's gate.
With every tear, we find a sign,
That love's great power will one day shine.

Bound by chains, yet hope ignites,
In darkest nights, the soul's true sights.
For in the struggle, we learn to rise,
With open hearts, we reach the skies.

When doubts assail, do not retreat,
For God walks here, where pain and prayer meet.
His grace shall lift, our spirits soar,
With breaking chains, we find our core.

The Pilgrimage of Sorrow

We walk the path of sorrow's dawn,
With heavy hearts, yet hope not gone.
Each step we take, a stone to bear,
A journey long, in fervent prayer.

In valleys low, we find the grace,
A gentle hand, in the stillest place.
Through tears we tread, yet light we find,
A compass set, on love's design.

The road is steep, but faith will guide,
In every trial, we shall abide.
For through our grief, new strength will rise,
In sacred trust, our spirits wise.

With every burden, a lesson learned,
In holy fire, our hearts once burned.
The pilgrimage of sorrow, sweet,
Will lead us home, where all hearts meet.

Pebbles on the Way to Glory

Each pebble speaks of trials past,
On paths of faith, when shadows cast.
They shape our steps, both small and grand,
In every stumble, we find His hand.

With weary feet, we tread the ground,
A journey long, where grace is found.
Each stone a mark, of battles fought,
In seeking truth, our souls are taught.

The road is rough, with twists and turns,
In every heart, a fire burns.
For every pebble, a lesson dear,
In hope's embrace, we conquer fear.

As we ascend, toward glory's gaze,
With faith in heart, we sing His praise.
These pebbles lead, where dreams take flight,
In love's embrace, we find the light.

The Garden of Grief

In a garden dark, where sorrows bloom,
Amidst the thorns, lies hidden room.
With tear-stained soil, we plant our seeds,
In hope's bright sun, the spirit feeds.

Each petal falls, a prayer released,
In every loss, our hearts increased.
For grief, though heavy, brings forth grace,
In gentle whispers, we find our place.

The fragrance sweet, of love once shared,
Through every ache, we know He cared.
In mourning's depth, new life will sprout,
In sacred space, we learn about.

The garden grows, with memories dear,
In every shadow, His presence near.
Through grief's embrace, we find the whole,
In tender moments, we heal the soul.

The Pilgrimage of the Afflicted

In shadows deep, they tread with care,
The afflicted souls, in whispered prayer.
Through valleys low, their burdens weigh,
Yet still they seek the light of day.

With every step, a faith reborn,
They carry scars, yet not forlorn.
Each trial faced, a lesson gained,
In every tear, a blessing drained.

The mountain high, a daunting climb,
But hope, their guide, transcends all time.
With hearts entwined, they march as one,
Together bound, till journey's done.

The road of pain, a sacred path,
Where love can heal and calm the wrath.
In kindred spirits, strength is found,
In every whisper, grace astound.

Oh, pilgrimage of those in need,
With every step, to faith we lead.
For through the night, the dawn shall break,
In every heart, a hope awake.

Blessed Be the Weary

Blessed be the weary soul,
Who finds in darkness, light's control.
With weary eyes and trembling hands,
They weave their dreams in sacred sands.

Though trials rage and shadows loom,
Within their hearts, the spirit blooms.
In every sigh, a prayer takes flight,
To seek the dawn, embrace the light.

The road ahead may twist and turn,
Yet in their hearts, a fire will burn.
With gentle grace, they bear their load,
On faith's sweet thread, they stake their road.

In blessed moments, find the peace,
Where weariness and grace release.
Their journey marked with love divine,
For in their souls, the stars align.

So blessed be the ones who strive,
With every breath, their hopes revive.
In weary paths, the truth shall gleam,
For in their hearts, the world redeems.

The Anvil of Adversity

In the anvil's heat, the metal bends,
Through trials faced, the spirit mends.
Each strike a testament to grace,
In hardened hearts, the truth we trace.

The forge of life, where shadows play,
In flames of pain, the soul finds sway.
Each moment carved, a lesson sown,
Through fire and storm, the strength is grown.

When burdens heavy weigh us down,
In silence loud, we lose our crown.
Yet in the struggle, beauty seeks,
As through the dark, the spirit speaks.

The anvil holds what time won't fade,
In the crucible, the soul is made.
With every challenge, bold and fierce,
We shape our fate, the heart's true pierce.

So let us rise from ashes gray,
In courage found, we'll find our way.
For in the trials, life does show,
The anvil's strength, the heart's pure glow.

Miracles in the Mending

In tender hands, the broken pieces lie,
With gentle grace, they learn to fly.
The healing balm that time adorns,
In every scar, a new heart born.

Through whispered prayers, the spirit hums,
In quiet moments, hope becomes.
The stitching of a life once torn,
Gives rise to dreams in light reborn.

With every tear, a lesson learned,
In darkness deep, the heart has yearned.
To mend the fabric, weave with care,
In every sigh, a soul laid bare.

In miracles, the heart finds grace,
Through trials faced, we find our place.
In every wound, a story told,
Of strength and love, both fierce and bold.

So let us gather, lost and found,
In healing's touch, our hopes surround.
For in the mending, life's light shines,
Miracles bloom in love's designs.

Resounding Silence

In the quiet night, whispers roam,
Silent prayers rise, seeking home.
Stars above, a celestial choir,
In stillness, hearts find sacred fire.

The echoes deep, a holy sound,
Within the void, love's light is found.
In every pause, grace will unfold,
Resounding truths that heal the cold.

In silence, souls gather near,
For in stillness, we persevere.
Each heartbeat, a drum of peace,
From burdens low, our sorrows cease.

Embrace the hush where spirits dwell,
In tender moments, we weave our spell.
For in the absence of noise and strife,
Lies the essence of sacred life.

So let us linger in this embrace,
In resounding silence, feel His grace.
For in the quiet, hope ignites,
In every shadow, love's light invites.

The Forge of Faith

In the fire's heat, souls are tried,
Through flames of doubt, our fears collide.
Yet in each spark, a promise glows,
The forge of faith, where courage grows.

With hammer's clang and iron's might,
Shapes our spirit in darkest night.
Each blow a test, each scar a sign,
In trials faced, our hearts align.

The anvil holds the dreams we seek,
In tempered strength, we find the weak.
For faith, like steel, requires the heat,
To forge a path, our spirits meet.

Through molten tears and shattered dreams,
We rise again, or so it seems.
In unity, we stand as one,
The forge of faith, our battles won.

With every trial, we learn to rise,
In the sacred fire, our hope complies.
So let us gather, strong and brave,
In the forge of faith, our souls we save.

Beneath the Weight of Woe

When shadows fall and burdens weigh,
Upon the heart, we find the way.
In mourning's grasp, we seek the light,
Beneath the weight, our spirits fight.

For every tear that traces grace,
A river flows in this holy place.
In sorrow deep, hope's roots will grow,
Strength arises, despite the woe.

The darkest nights will pass like mist,
Each moment held, a gentle twist.
In pain, we find a call to prayer,
A bond of love that we must share.

Together we walk through valleys low,
In unity, the light will show.
For every load that we must bear,
In hearts entwined, we find our prayer.

So let us gather, hand in hand,
Through the trials, let us stand.
For beneath the weight, love will bestow,
A peace eternal, despite the woe.

Songs of the Grieving Heart

In quiet rooms, where echoes dwell,
The songs of grief begin to swell.
Each note a whisper, soft and clear,
In aching hearts, we draw you near.

With every chord, a memory sings,
Of love once lost and fleeting things.
In sorrow's arms, we find our place,
A melody of divine grace.

Through tears we sing, a sacred vow,
To honor those whose love we plow.
In grief's embrace, we find the art,
Of healing wounds that touch the heart.

For in the pain, our voices rise,
A symphony that never dies.
In every loss, a thread of hope,
A tapestry that helps us cope.

So let us sing, though tears may flow,
In harmony, we weave and sow.
For songs of the grieving heart impart,
A love eternal, a beat divine art.

The Harmony of Endless Hope

In the whispers of the night, we pray,
Stars above guide our way.
In shadows deep, faith will gleam,
Hope's light ignites every dream.

Through trials fierce, hearts entwined,
In love divine, solace we find.
With every breath, we rise anew,
In harmony, our spirits grew.

Mountains tall and valleys low,
In every struggle, strength will flow.
With open hearts, our burdens shared,
In endless hope, we feel prepared.

Hands uplifted, souls aligned,
In unity, true peace we find.
The waters calm, the storms subside,
In faith, we shall abide.

Let every tear fall to the ground,
In every sorrow, love is found.
In the melody of grace we sing,
Together, hope will always spring.

The Serpent and the Sage

In the garden where truth lays bare,
A serpent coils with cunning flair.
The sage stands firm, wisdom bright,
In shadows dark, he brings the light.

Temptations whisper, soft and sweet,
Yet steadfast is the sage's feet.
With every choice, a path unfolds,
In silence deep, the story holds.

Life's lessons wrapped in sinuous guise,
Through trials faced, the spirit flies.
For in each struggle, treasures lie,
The serpent's wisdom lifts us high.

With gentle words, the sage will guide,
Through tangled woods, we shall abide.
In knowledge vast, we find our way,
The serpent's dance will not dismay.

From shadows cast, to light we strive,
In the heart of truth, we come alive.
Each step we take, a choice divine,
In every moment, love will shine.

Resurrection Through Ruin

From ashes deep, a flower blooms,
In darkest nights, the light consumes.
Through shattered dreams and fading breath,
Life finds a way beyond mere death.

The soil rich with trials sown,
In every fall, our fate is grown.
With every tear, a seed is cast,
In resurrection, shadows past.

Hope emerges from the ground,
In brokenness, new strength is found.
The path of pain, a sacred rite,
In ruins raw, we gain our sight.

Through storms we face, the spirit soars,
In every struggle, wisdom pours.
The dawn arises, veils are torn,
In light reborn, we greet the morn.

With open hearts and hands that lift,
In every loss, a precious gift.
From ruins vast, we rise again,
In faith renewed, we will ascend.

Grace Found in the Grind

In daily toil, where shadows creep,
Through labor's weight, our spirits leap.
With every challenge, lessons clear,
In humble strength, we persevere.

Though weary bones may ache and moan,
In the grind, the seeds are sown.
With every step, we forge our fate,
In grace, we trust, and elevate.

The beauty found in simple tasks,
In each small act, the spirit basks.
Through sweat and tears, we carve our path,
In daily grinds, we find our math.

With hearts aflame, on journeys steep,
In the work we do, our dreams we keep.
Each moment cherished, nothing small,
In grace, we rise, we answer the call.

So lift your hands, embrace the day,
In work divine, we find our way.
For in the grind, a truth resides,
In grace, our soul forever abides.

The Whisper of Resilience

In the quiet corners of the soul,
A whisper stirs, a gentle call.
Through trials dark, it leads the way,
A light that guides through night and day.

With every fall, we learn to rise,
From ashes, filled with hopeful sighs.
In storms that rage, we stand our ground,
In faith and strength, our hearts are found.

The mountain's peak, so hard to scale,
Yet in the climb, our spirits sail.
With every step, we find our grace,
Through whispered words, we seek His face.

Resilience blooms in barren land,
A testament to faith's strong hand.
With every tear, a seed is sown,
In sacred soil, our strength has grown.

Together we weave a tapestry,
Of courage, love, and piety.
In unity, we face the strife,
The whisper of resilience, our life.

From Shadows to Sanctity

In shadows deep where fears reside,
A flicker of light begins to guide.
Through whispered prayers and hopeful seams,
We journey forth to find our dreams.

From darkness lost, a spark ignites,
Transforming pain into sacred sights.
With every step upon this ground,
We rise from ashes, sanctified, found.

The heart that opens, fears confess,
In sacred space, we find our rest.
Each breath a hymn, each sigh a plea,
In the light of love, we set spirits free.

In every trial, a lesson clear,
From shadows cast, we draw near.
With faith as armor, love as sword,
We walk the path, our hearts restored.

Together, we seek a brighter dawn,
With hands held high, we move along.
From shadows deep to sanctity,
A sacred dance, our souls set free.

The Gift of Grief

In sorrow's embrace, we find the grace,
A gift wrapped tight in time and space.
Through tears that fall, we learn to see,
The beauty held in grief's decree.

Each moment lost, a cry for love,
A whispered prayer to skies above.
In every ache, the heart expands,
Connecting us with gentle hands.

The weight of loss, a heavy shroud,
Yet in its depth, we stand unbowed.
For in the silence, wisdom speaks,
A lesson learned in tender peaks.

Through grief we grow, we come alive,
In memory, the spirit thrives.
Each heartbeat echoes those we've known,
In love's embrace, we're never alone.

So we gather strength from what we've lost,
In every tear, love pays the cost.
The gift of grief, a sacred tune,
In darkest nights, we find our moon.

A Dance Among the Damned

In shadows cast, the lost do sway,
A dance of souls, both night and day.
In every heartbeat, echoes ring,
A melody of suffering.

Yet in the dark, a spark ignites,
Redemption found in desperate fights.
We waltz with fears, embrace the pain,
In every step, lessons remain.

The cursed and broken, hand in hand,
Together rise to make a stand.
For love persists in realms of night,
A beacon shining, fierce and bright.

In chaos spun, a sacred rhyme,
We find our truth beyond the grime.
Through fractured paths, we learn to flow,
In unity, our spirits grow.

So let us dance amidst the strife,
With every twirl, reclaim our life.
Among the damned, our hearts will sing,
A dance of hope, in shadows spring.

Angels in Our Darkness

In shadows deep, they softly tread,
With whispers sweet, they calm our dread.
Wings of mercy, they spread so wide,
Guiding souls on the darkened tide.

In nights of sorrow, they hold our fears,
With gentle grace, they dry our tears.
Their light a beacon, forever near,
In the silence, we feel them clear.

Through storms of life, they lend their might,
In moments lost, they bring us light.
They carry hope upon their backs,
In every trial, they fill the cracks.

With every prayer, a song ascends,
To the heavens where love transcends.
Angels watch as we strive to cope,
Through their presence, we find our hope.

So let us lift our hearts in praise,
For angels guide our weary ways.
In every heartache, they surely dwell,
Woven with love, they weave their spell.

Light After Tribulation

In valleys low, the trials rise,
Yet faith endures, for hope complies.
Through darkest nights, we strive to see,
The dawn that waits, so faithfully.

Upon the cross, we bear the weight,
Yet know that love will not abate.
For every tear, a promise made,
In strength we walk, our fears allayed.

When storms may roar and shadows loom,
We grasp the light that breaks the gloom.
In every struggle, we find a way,
To rise anew with each new day.

The sun will shine on paths once gray,
As we ascend from disarray.
With grateful hearts, we sing our song,
For in the light, we all belong.

Through tribulation, souls refine,
Emerging strong, forever shine.
In unity, we stand as one,
Guided onward by the Son.

The Testament of Suffering

In quiet hours, we bear the pain,
Each wound a mark, a sacred chain.
Yet from the ashes, hope will rise,
A testament beneath the skies.

Through trials fierce, we meet the night,
With every struggle, we seek the light.
In every heart, a garden sown,
Of grace and strength, in seeds well-known.

For suffering molds the soul's true form,
And in the tempest, we find our norm.
With faith as shield, we stand our ground,
In darkest moments, love is found.

A hymn of courage, we shall sing,
For every burden's a holy thing.
In trials endured, we grow aware,
Of blessings whispered in the air.

So let our prayers rise from the pain,
And in our hearts, let love remain.
For in the struggle, we are not lost,
We rise as one, despite the cost.

A Martyr's Song of Survival

Upon the flame, our spirits soar,
In sacrifice, we find the core.
With every heartbeat, a tale unfolds,
Of courage written in the bold.

In darkest nights, we stand our ground,
In whispered prayers, our strength is found.
With steadfast hearts, we face the tide,
Through trials faced, we do not hide.

With faith as armor, we brave the storm,
For love ignites a sacred form.
From ashes rise, a radiant glow,
A testament to seeds we sow.

With every breath, we speak our truth,
A melody of eternal youth.
In every struggle, we hear the call,
Of martyr's song, uniting all.

So let our voices echo wide,
In every heart, our hope reside.
Through trials faced, we shall survive,
Together bound, we feel alive.

The Broken Halo

In the silence, whispers sigh,
A halo dims, but does not die.
In shattered light, our faith shall stand,
Guided by His gentle hand.

Wounds may bleed, and hearts may ache,
Yet through the pain, there's hope awake.
With every tear, a prayer we weave,
In brokenness, we learn to believe.

Beyond the veil, a promise gleams,
Restoration found in fractured dreams.
The Lord, our healer, tenderly calls,
He lifts us high, despite our falls.

We gather strength from shadows cast,
In every trial, a testament vast.
Though the halo hangs by a thread,
With faith unyielding, we are led.

So let us rise, in grace we'll tread,
For love persists where hope has bled.
In broken halos, light shines clear,
With hearts entwined, we cast out fear.

Grace Amidst the Thorns

In fields of thorns, where sorrows grow,
The seeds of grace begin to show.
Amidst the trials, a flower blooms,
A fragrant hope in darkest rooms.

With each sharp pain, a lesson learned,
In moments bleak, our spirits turned.
For every thorn that pricks the skin,
A gentle grace resides within.

In shadows deep, we find our song,
The melody where we belong.
With every step through thorny ways,
We lift our hearts in thankful praise.

Through suffering's veil, a light appears,
It chases far away our fears.
The thorns may sting, but we shall rise,
With faith as wings, we touch the skies.

So let us dance among the pain,
For in the thorns, His love we gain.
Grace intertwines with every test,
In thorns of life, we find our rest.

Sanctuary in Suffering

In quiet corners, pain may dwell,
Yet in our hearts, a sacred well.
Each tear a drop, a prayerful plea,
A sanctuary, where souls are free.

Through tempest winds and shadows cast,
We find our shelter, hope steadfast.
In suffering's grasp, we learn to soar,
Embracing trials, we seek much more.

The burdens heavy, yet grace unfurls,
A gentle whisper that speaks to worlds.
Within our pain, divine embrace,
In suffering's grip, we find our space.

For in the dark, the light still shines,
A flicker bright, where love entwines.
Each moment bitter, a chance to grow,
A sanctuary in suffering, we know.

So let us gather, hand in hand,
A community where hope can stand.
In every heart, a sacred place,
A sanctuary of eternal grace.

The Light in Our Shadows

In every shadow, whispers dwell,
A light transcends, a sacred spell.
In darkness deep, we dare to see,
The radiant grace that sets us free.

Through trials fierce and burdens wide,
In seeking Him, we turn the tide.
For even in the night's embrace,
His gentle light, our hearts efface.

The struggles fierce, they shape our soul,
With every fall, we find our goal.
In light's soft glow, despair will fade,
In shadows' clutch, our hope is made.

With every flicker, love ignites,
A testament to brighter nights.
In darkest times, we glean the truth,
The light within, our living proof.

So let us rise, with faith anew,
Embracing light, our paths pursue.
In shadows thick, we shall proclaim,
The light in our hearts, ignites the flame.

Divinity in the Dark

In shadows deep, a whisper calls,
The light of grace, it softly falls.
In trials faced, the spirit grows,
A sacred peace in silence glows.

Through midnight's veil, the heart shall find,
A presence strong, so pure, divine.
In every tear, a seed of hope,
A promise held, we learn to cope.

The stars above, they shine so bright,
Reminders of eternal light.
In darkest times, we find our way,
With faith our guide, we choose to stay.

Each lonely hour, a prayer raises,
To heaven's grace, it softly praises.
For in the night, we learn to see,
The beauty born of mystery.

So take my hand, and walk with me,
Through shadowed paths, to set us free.
In divinity, we find our spark,
A flame of hope within the dark.

The Sanctuary of Suffering

In the silence of our pain,
We seek the light amidst the rain.
Our burdens heavy, hearts so sore,
Yet in this place, we're called for more.

Beneath the weight, a strength we find,
Through trials, love is redefined.
The sanctuary where we bleed,
Gives birth to hope, a gentle seed.

Each tear that falls, a sacred gift,
In suffering's grip, the spirits lift.
The aching heart unveils the soul,
A longing deep to be made whole.

Together we shall bear the weight,
For all the storms will never break.
In unity, we offer praise,
In suffering's end, our faith will blaze.

The sanctuary holds our cries,
In darkest nights, our spirits rise.
Through every wound, a chance to heal,
For love's embrace is truly real.

Grace Among Thorns

Amongst the thorns, a rose does grow,
Its beauty shines, a radiant glow.
In harshest trials, grace appears,
A balm for all our deepest fears.

The prick of pain, a lesson learned,
In every flame, the heart is burned.
Yet in this fire, we find our song,
In weakness, we become so strong.

With every thorn, we stand anew,
Embracing love in all we do.
For grace abounds in darkest nights,
A guiding star, our hope ignites.

So let the thorns be not our end,
But pathways where the spirit bends.
In every struggle, lift your eyes,
For grace awaits beyond the skies.

Together in this thorny maze,
We walk in faith, through trials we graze.
With hearts ablaze, we rise and soar,
For love's sweet truth is evermore.

The Altar of Endurance

Upon the altar, we lay our fears,
In silent prayers, we shed our tears.
Through trials long, our spirits rise,
A testament to love that ties.

Endurance carved in every scar,
A journey long, yet never far.
For in each step, the heart expands,
Held by the grace of guiding hands.

With every dawn, we greet the fight,
In shadows cast, we seek the light.
The altar stands, a place to meet,
Where burdens lifted find their seat.

Together, where our stories blend,
A sacred bond that will not end.
In shared despair, we find the flame,
No longer lost, we speak His name.

So let us rise upon this ground,
In every heartbeat, love is found.
The altar calls with strength anew,
In endurance, we begin anew.

Cadence of the Heartbroken

In shadows deep, the heart does cry,
Whispers of love that drift and die.
Yet in the night, a flicker shines,
A balm for wounds, where hope entwines.

The tears may flow, like rivers wide,
In aching silence, the soul confides.
Yet faith stands firm, a guiding light,
That turns the dark into the bright.

A promise lingers in the air,
Love's ember glows, beyond despair.
With every beat, the heart does mend,
In loss we find, the strength to bend.

In every whisper, a prayer rises,
To the heavens' vast, unseen disguises.
Through broken echoes, love will soar,
And in the pain, we learn to adore.

So hold the heart, though shattered still,
For in its cracks, we find our will.
A melody born from silent sighs,
In through the shadows, the spirit flies.

Faith's Forge in Fire

In trials faced, our spirits grow,
Through flames of doubt, we learn to know.
The heat reveals, what's pure and bright,
Forging strength in the darkest night.

With every spark, a lesson learned,
In every loss, a heart has yearned.
Through bitter pain, our souls ignite,
A beacon shining through endless night.

As ashes fall, seeds find the ground,
In barren places, hope is found.
Faith's gentle hand, it guides the way,
To brighter tomorrows, come what may.

With every tear, a prayer ascends,
In every moment, the heart transcends.
Through trials faced, we stand as one,
In faith's embrace, we rise, reborn.

So take the heat, let it refine,
For in the fire, we learn to shine.
An ember glows with purpose clear,
In faith's strong forge, we conquer fear.

Echoes of the Weary Soul

In weary nights, the heart does sigh,
Beneath the stars, where shadows lie.
Each echo whispers tales of strife,
Yet speaks of hope, the pulse of life.

With every breath, the soul takes flight,
In search of peace, in quest of light.
Through valleys deep, and mountains high,
The spirit wanders, asking why.

Yet in the silence, a truth unfolds,
A gentle hand, that never scolds.
In every doubt, faith softly calls,
To lift the soul when darkness falls.

Through tears we find, the way to heal,
In sacred silence, joy we feel.
With every tune, the heart's refrain,
An echo sweet, that soothes the pain.

So let the weary find their rest,
In arms of love, forever blessed.
For in the echoes, we find our part,
The sacred song that binds the heart.

The Silent Prayer of Grief

In quiet shadows, sorrow dwells,
A silent prayer, the spirit tells.
With every breath, a memory sighs,
In depths of night, where longing lies.

The heartache speaks, though words may fail,
In stillness found, the spirit wails.
Yet in the silence, hope can bloom,
A light that dances, dispelling gloom.

Through every tear, a story lives,
Of love once shared, the heart forgives.
In tender moments, grief reveals,
The sacred bond that never seals.

With every dawn, the pain subsides,
In memories sweet, the heart abides.
Together held, though apart we stand,
In grief's embrace, we understand.

So let the tears fall like gentle rain,
Each drop a prayer, each moment, gain.
In silent grief, we find our way,
To honor love, day by day.

A Testament of Tears

In the stillness of night, we weep,
A whisper of heartache, deep.
Every tear, a prayer sent high,
To the heavens, where angels sigh.

Each drop a story, sacred and true,
Reflecting the pain we've been through.
In sorrow's embrace, we find our way,
With faith as our anchor, we pray.

The weight of the world, we bear on our backs,
Yet grace intercedes, filling the cracks.
In mourning we gather, a tapestry spun,
Binding our wounds, we are never done.

Wounds become wisdom, in time's gentle hands,
A testament forged in divine strands.
Through trials and tears, we rise like the dawn,
In God's tender mercy, we are reborn.

Let each tear fall, a lesson to learn,
In the furnace of faith, our spirits will burn.
For love's gentle light, we shall always strive,
In the heart's darkest hour, hope will survive.

Wounds Woven in Light

In the fabric of life, we wear our scars,
Each thread a reminder, healing from wars.
With hands intertwined, we journey the night,
Finding solace in wounds woven in light.

From shadows emerge, the lessons of old,
In the warmth of compassion, our hearts unfold.
In the silence, we listen for truths yet to find,
With whispered affirmations, we're gently aligned.

The tapestry glimmers with colors of grace,
Every sorrow embraced in love's warm embrace.
For healing comes softly, like dew on the grass,
As we gather our strength, the shadows will pass.

In moments of stillness, our spirits shall soar,
With faith as our guide, we'll open each door.
For every bruise, there's a story anew,
And in wounds woven lightly, we find the true hue.

Embrace the journey, let faith be your song,
In the light of the heart, we truly belong.
Together we rise, as the dawn breaks in bloom,
In wounds woven in light, we cast out the gloom.

The Garden of Grief

In the garden of grief, flowers bloom bright,
With petals of sorrow, kissed by the night.
Amongst the thorns, a fragrance of love,
Reminding us always, we're cradled above.

In the soil of our hearts, we plant every tear,
With faith in the harvest, the healing draws near.
Each moment of anguish, a chance to renew,
In the garden of grief, life's essence shines through.

The sun through the clouds, brings warmth to our souls,
As we nurture our wounds, their bittersweet roles.
For in every loss, a memory remains,
A garden of grief, where love never wanes.

Let us gather the blossoms, share stories untold,
In unity blooming, a vision of gold.
For together we rise, amidst shadows and strife,
In the garden of grief, we celebrate life.

With tenderness woven in each whispered prayer,
We acknowledge the struggle, the weight that we bear.
For in love's embrace, we'll always find peace,
In the garden of grief, our spirits release.

When the Heart Cries Out

When the heart cries out, the heavens will hear,
A symphony of hope, transcending our fear.
In the depths of despair, we find strength anew,
With whispers of faith, the spirit breaks through.

Each cry is a call to the solace divine,
From the ashes of sorrow, our souls intertwine.
In the tempest of anguish, we find solid ground,
As we gather our voices, a harmony found.

Let the heart cry out, let the tears freely flow,
For in every heartbeat, love's essence will grow.
With compassion as warmth, we'll tend to each flame,
In the chorus of healing, we call out Your name.

From darkness to dawn, through valleys so deep,
With faith as our anchor, our promises keep.
When the heart cries out, it's a melody sweet,
In the rhythm of grace, our spirits shall meet.

So let every moment of pain sing aloud,
In the face of the storm, we stand unbowed.
For when the heart cries out, love's answer is near,
In the echoes of anguish, our purpose is clear.

The Crossroads of Trial

In the silence, we stand at a fork,
Hearts heavy with the weight of the walk.
Divine whispers stir in the air,
Guiding our feet through the depths of despair.

Paths divided, yet one leads to grace,
With faith, we gather, in this sacred space.
Doubts may linger, shadows of night,
But light breaks forth with the dawn's early light.

Each step is woven with trust, not seen,
The trail may be rugged, but hearts stay keen.
When we falter, the spirit will cry,
To lean on His love, to never say die.

In the struggle, we find our true song,
With trials faced, we become ever strong.
Embrace the journey where trials reside,
For every crossroad brings hope as our guide.

Breaths of the Burdened

In the shadows, burdens take form,
Yet through the night, His love keeps us warm.
Each breath a prayer, whispered unheard,
Carried on wings of our deepest word.

Awash with tears, yet faith will not cease,
In every struggle, the heart finds peace.
Pain may accompany, a friend on the way,
For through the sorrows, we learn how to pray.

With shoulders weighed down, we reach for the skies,
For in the darkness, the spirit will rise.
Breaths of the burdened, yet light shines within,
Through trials we conquer, let new life begin.

Each moment a step, forgotten and frail,
But together we journey, our hopes never pale.
In the depths of the night, faith will ignite,
With breaths of the burdened, we rise to the light.

Beauty Born from Bruises

In the cracks of our hearts, where pain finds its voice,
Beauty emerges, and we learn to rejoice.
Through trials endured, our spirits withstand,
Bruises tell stories by divine hand.

Each wound is a canvas, an artwork of grace,
Crafted in darkness, we find our true place.
Resilience blooms where sorrow has trod,
In the garden of hope, nurtured by God.

With scars that we carry, we learn to forgive,
For life's sweetest lessons lead us how to live.
Emerging from shadows, we rise from the falls,
Embracing our bruises, we answer the calls.

A tapestry woven of love and of strife,
In the story of pain, we discover true life.
So take heart, for beauty from bruises does grow,
In the heart of this darkness, let your light show.

The Ascent of the Exiled

On mountains of sorrow, we tread with care,
Exiled from comfort, yet not alone there.
With each staggered step, we find purpose anew,
Guided by faith, where our spirits break through.

The summit ahead, though rugged the climb,
We find strength in struggle, transcending time.
The echoes of trials bring lessons to share,
As we tread on the path, divinely aware.

With hands held in prayer, we rise with the dawn,
Though weary and worn, our hopes carry on.
Echoes of laughter mingle with pain,
In the ascent of exiles, our hearts learn to reign.

Each step a reminder of grace found within,
Through trials and tribulations, new life will begin.
The journey is sacred, though burdened we roam,
In the ascent of the exiled, we find our true home.

The Call of the Enduring

In shadows deep, we find our light,
A whisper calls, through darkest night.
With faith as armor, hearts made bold,
We heed the call, as love unfolds.

Through trials faced, we rise anew,
Each step we take, a path so true.
In every tear, a seed is sown,
In every loss, our strength has grown.

As storms may rage, we stand our ground,
With hope entwined, our souls are surrounded.
Together we walk, hand in hand,
In the great design, we understand.

The journey long, yet grace we share,
In unity, we find our prayer.
Emerging bright, from trials faced,
For love is here, and hope embraced.

So let the world with noise resound,
Our hearts in peace, through chaos found.
The call of life, through joy and pain,
Enduring souls, we shall remain.

Healed by the Journey

Through winding roads, our spirits grow,
In every step, a chance to know.
The burdens carried, turned to grace,
Healed by love, in time and space.

With every heartache and each trial,
We gather strength, a sacred smile.
In open arms, the world receives,
The beauty found in hearts that believe.

We seek the light in darkest days,
In whispers soft, the heart obeys.
Each moment shared, a freedom gained,
In healing waters, we are sustained.

The path we walk is lined with prayer,
With grace bestowed, we find repair.
Through every storm, and every tear,
Life's journey leads us ever near.

The scars we bear, tell stories bold,
In every crack, our hope unfolds.
Healed by the journey, we rise again,
In love's embrace, we find our zen.

Refined by the Flames

In passions' glow, we learn to rise,
Through trials faced, our spirits wise.
Refined by fire, our souls ignite,
In sacred embers, we find our light.

Each challenge met, a chance for growth,
Through flames we forge, our sacred oath.
The heat may burn, but not destroy,
For in the struggle, we find our joy.

The ashes fall, yet seeds are sown,
In fiery depths, our strength is honed.
Transformation's gift, a sacred claim,
From once lost paths, we rise in flame.

With every blaze, our hearts unite,
In the dance of life, we find our flight.
Oh, precious flames, that cleanse and mend,
Refined in love, we rise again.

So let the fire burn and shine,
For in its warmth, our souls align.
Refined by flames, our spirits soar,
In love's embrace, forevermore.

The Veil of Vulnerability

In tender hearts, the truth revealed,
Behind the veil, our souls unsealed.
A fragile dance, of love and fear,
In vulnerability, we draw near.

When walls come down, the heart beats free,
In every shared tear, humility.
We find our strength, in openness true,
In gentle whispers, love breaks through.

Embrace the scars, for they do tell,
Of battles fought, we know too well.
In honesty, our souls unite,
In vulnerability, we find our light.

The courage blooms in hearts laid bare,
In every moment, a chance to care.
With arms wide open, we face the day,
Through the veil of love, we find our way.

So let us stand, with hearts exposed,
In every truth, our love composed.
The veil reveals, that we are whole,
In vulnerability, we find our soul.

The Crucible of Hope

In shadows deep where spirits weep,
A flame ignites, a promise keeps.
Through trials faced, our hearts entwine,
In crucibles, our souls refine.

The aching night gives way to dawn,
With every tear, the light is drawn.
In faith we rise, as gold through fire,
Our spirits blaze, our hearts aspire.

When doubts arise, and voices leer,
In silence found, we conquer fear.
With hands held high, we seek the sky,
In unity, we soar and fly.

Through storms we tread, anchored in grace,
For every trial, we find our place.
A sacred bond ignites our spark,
As hope's embrace dispels the dark.

In love we trust, our beacon true,
A guiding light in all we do.
On paths unknown, we walk as one,
In crucibles of hope, we've begun.

Prayers on Wounded Knees

In humble grace before the throne,
We bow our heads, our hearts alone.
With whispered prayers in aching pleas,
The spirit moves on wounded knees.

Each tear a gem, each sigh a prayer,
In quiet depths, we find You there.
Amongst our pain, we seek Your face,
In trials, Lord, we find Your grace.

With burdens heavy, we seek release,
In sacred trust, we find our peace.
Though shadows cast and doubts arise,
In fervent cries, our hope defies.

The world may shake, the heart may quake,
But on our knees, our faith won't break.
Every whisper becomes a song,
In every struggle, we grow strong.

Lord, hear our prayers, our hearts laid bare,
In love, we rise through every snare.
With steadfast hearts, we journey forth,
On wounded knees, we find our worth.

The Quests of the Scarred

In every wound, a story told,
Of battles fought, and hearts made bold.
Through scars that mar, the light breaks in,
A testament of where we've been.

From trials faced, resilience blooms,
In shattered dreams, our spirit zooms.
Through weary nights and storms of pain,
We seek the sun, the hope we gain.

Our journeys lead through valleys low,
Yet from the dark, our courage grows.
With every step, we find our way,
In quests of old, we mold the day.

In fellowship, our spirits bind,
A tapestry of souls aligned.
With hearts of fire, we dare to dream,
In scarred lives, we find the stream.

So let us rise from ashes gray,
With courage fierce, we'll light the way.
Together bold, through trials steered,
In quests of the scarred, we are revered.

The Stone that Breaks the Jail

In darkness bound, our spirits sigh,
A heavy weight beneath the sky.
Yet stones of faith, they pave the way,
In walls of hurt, we find our say.

The chains may rattle, fears may grow,
But hope, a seed, begins to sow.
With every prayer, the stones may shift,
In strength divine, we find our gift.

Each cry for help, a voice that calls,
To break the silence of these walls.
With courage found in unity,
The stone breaks chains, we are set free.

In faith, we build, in trials strong,
For every right, there must be wrong.
A shattered cell, a heart made whole,
In faith's embrace, we find our soul.

So let us rise, though faint and frail,
Together, love will never fail.
For hope is found where stones may lay,
The stone that breaks the jail, we pray.

The Weight of Faith

In shadows deep, the spirit aches,
Yet light shall break through weary wakes.
With whispered prayers, we reach above,
Embracing grace, a gift of love.

Mountains tremble, valleys kneel,
In every heart, the truth we feel.
The heavy load, yet we shall rise,
With faith that spans the endless skies.

So cast your doubts into the sea,
And let the dawn set your heart free.
For burdens fade in light of day,
With faith to guide, we find our way.

In trials faced, our courage grows,
A nurturing breeze, the spirit flows.
In every tear, a lesson learned,
The flame of faith shall always burn.

Together we walk this sacred road,
With faith as our shield, we share the load.
In unity, our hearts shall soar,
Upon the wings of love once more.

Chains of the Suffering Heart

In darkest night, the heart does cry,
For burdens born, we question why.
Yet in the pain, a truth shall gleam,
A flicker of hope, a fragile dream.

These chains we wear, they bind us tight,
Yet through the tears, we seek the light.
For every wound, a chance to heal,
A sacred dance, the soul's reveal.

So cling to faith, though trials ensue,
For in our strife, we're born anew.
The path of thorns shall lead us hence,
To gardens rich in recompense.

In every sorrow, love shall rise,
Transcending pain, we touch the skies.
The chains may rattle, yet we stand,
With open hearts, we join hands.

In suffering's grip, we find our grace,
A deeper truth we must embrace.
So wear your chains, but lift your gaze,
For love endures through endless days.

The Alchemy of Affliction

Within the fire of the soul's own strife,
We learn the art of living life.
For every test, a spark ignites,
Transforming darkness into lights.

The crucible of pain we face,
Turns lead to gold, a sacred space.
In trials met, the spirit grows,
A deeper strength within us flows.

With each rough stone, we carve our fate,
Our hearts embrace what we create.
The alchemy of loss and gain,
Unveils the beauty found in pain.

So hold the sorrow, let it teach,
For through our wounds, the soul will reach.
In every tear, a gem appears,
A testament to all our years.

In life's great forge, we shall not break,
For love prevails, and hearts awake.
The alchemy of grief shall lead,
To hope renewed, and hearts set free.

In Quietude of the Soul

In silence deep, where whispers dwell,
The soul finds peace, a sacred well.
With gentle breaths, we seek the space,
Where love's embrace becomes our grace.

The world around may rage and roar,
Yet in stillness, we find our core.
In quietude, the heart shall bloom,
Transforming darkness into room.

With every thought, a prayer takes flight,
In solitude, we chase the light.
The soul's reflection, calm and bright,
Awakens wisdom, clears the night.

So linger here, where time does pause,
A moment's rest, without a cause.
In quietude, the spirit sings,
Unraveling the joy that stillness brings.

In tender silence, hear the call,
Of love that binds, embracing all.
For in our hearts, the truth shall glow,
In quietude, our spirits grow.

The Altar of Endurance

Upon the altar, steadfast prayers rise,
Hearts lifted high, seeking the skies.
Every burden laid at the feet of grace,
In trials and storms, we find our place.

With faith as our shield, we face the night,
Each tear a tribute, each struggle a rite.
In shadows we wander, yet never alone,
For in every battle, His love is our throne.

Through whispers of doubt, His voice is clear,
In the silence of pain, He draws ever near.
With whispers of hope, we rise once more,
Emboldened by truth, our spirits soar.

When weariness weighs like an anchor's chain,
The altar of endurance eases our strain.
Though the path be rugged, we will not fall,
In the heart of the storm, we hear the call.

For each step taken with courage and grace,
Fulfills the promise of this sacred space.
United in spirit, we stand and fight,
At the altar of endurance, we find our light.

Faith's Unyielding Embrace

In the stillness, faith softly speaks,
To weary hearts, it soothes and seeks.
With every heartbeat, it whispers near,
In shadows of doubt, faith conquers fear.

Embrace the promise that dawn will break,
From ashes and ruins, new life we make.
With hands clasped tightly, our spirits soar,
Faith's unyielding embrace opens every door.

Though trials may come like a thief in the night,
In the depth of darkness, we'll find the light.
With prayer as our armor, we stand our ground,
In faith's sweet embrace, true hope is found.

With every stumble, He holds our hand,
Guiding our steps upon shifting sand.
In moments of struggle, when courage wanes,
Faith's unyielding embrace sustains and reigns.

So let us rise, together entwined,
With hearts knitted close, our souls aligned.
In the tapestry of love, we'll shine and blaze,
In faith's unyielding embrace, we'll forever praise.

The Blessing of Bruises

In the tender grip of pain, we grow,
Each bruise a lesson, each scar a glow.
In valleys of heartache, the spirit expands,
The blessing of bruises guides gentle hands.

With every stumble on the path we tread,
Comes fortitude woven through words unsaid.
In the depths of struggle, we learn to stand,
In the blessing of bruises, we find His hand.

Like diamonds emerging from pressure's hold,
Our faith crystallizes, our stories unfold.
For every tear shed in sorrow's embrace,
There lies a blessing, a sacred space.

In trials that bend but never break,
We find the strength that love will make.
With every bruise, our hearts awaken,
The blessing of bruises, a promise unshaken.

So let us cherish the pain we endure,
For in our struggles, we find the pure.
A tapestry woven with darkness and light,
The blessing of bruises, our soul's true fight.

Requiem of Resilience

In the echo of silence, resilience sings,
A requiem soft for the hope that it brings.
Through trials and storms, our spirits ignite,
A symphony woven from darkness to light.

With each breath taken in courage and grace,
We rise from the ashes, fear cannot trace.
In the heart of struggle, our spirits align,
A requiem of resilience, forever divine.

Through valleys of sorrow, our voices will soar,
For the strength of our hearts opens every door.
We gather together, each hand held tight,
In the requiem of resilience, we claim our right.

Each note of our story a chord of the brave,
Resilience echoes, bringing hope to the grave.
In the depths of despair, our light will remain,
A requiem of resilience that conquers pain.

So let us rejoice in the battles we've fought,
For every wound cherished, every lesson taught.
In unity strong, our voices unite,
In the requiem of resilience, we find our light.

Embracing the Broken

In shadows deep, where hope seems lost,
We gather 'round the weary cost.
With hands outstretched, we lift the frayed,
And find the strength in hearts betrayed.

The fractured souls, we hold so dear,
In tender grace, we shed each tear.
For in the cracks, the light shall seep,
A promise made, our love to keep.

Together we rise, from dust to dawn,
In every weakness, we are reborn.
For every heart that feels alone,
Embraced by love, we're never known.

With shattered dreams, we weave our song,
In God's warm embrace, we all belong.
Through every trial and anguished plea,
The broken spirit finds its plea.

So let us walk this path of grace,
In every heart, a sacred space.
For in the dark, His light will shine,
Together, brokenness divine.

Reflections of Affliction

In quiet moments of despair,
We lift our eyes; we lay our care.
Each wound a mark, each scar a tale,
In faith we stand, though shadows pale.

From valleys low to mountains high,
Let every tear become a sigh.
In suffering's grip, we seek the balm,
A holy peace that stills the storm.

The trials we face are not in vain,
For through the trials, we shall gain.
In every heart, a seed is sown,
Transforming pain to strength we've grown.

With every burden, we rise anew,
In each dark night, His light breaks through.
In scars we find, reflections pure,
A promise kept, a love secure.

As mirrors held to heaven's grace,
We find Him there, we find our place.
In every dark, a dawn will break,
Through every grief, new paths we make.

The Pilgrim's Pain

Along the path of twisted fate,
The pilgrim walks, though trials mate.
With every step, the heart does scream,
Yet in the struggle, grows the dream.

The road is long, the light is dim,
But trust in Him, our hope won't swim.
For in the pain, our spirits yearn,
In weary hearts, His fire burns.

Through tempest winds, we cry and plead,
Yet in the silence, He plants the seed.
For every tear, a lesson learned,
In every fall, to Him we turn.

So let the journey dance with grace,
In wandering steps, we seek His face.
For in our pain, we claim the way,
The pilgrim's heart, forever sway.

In every shadow, trust the light,
For pain is but a fleeting night.
In each embrace, let courage rise,
The pilgrim walks, where love defies.

Resilient Reverence

In every storm, we stand as one,
With hearts uplifted, battles won.
Each trial faced, a sacred rite,
Resilient souls, we embrace the fight.

In whispered prayers, we find our core,
Through trembling hands, we seek for more.
With gratitude, we raise our song,
In every note, we find where we belong.

The strength we draw from faith unbending,
In every heart, His love is lending.
Through fractured days, we lift our gaze,
In reverence, we walk through haze.

In stillness found, our spirits soar,
With every breath, we yearn for more.
For in our weakness, grace is found,
In every setback, love abounds.

So join the choir of hearts so brave,
In every voice, a hymn to save.
Resilient reverence, our holy claim,
With every struggle, we bled the same.

Wings Made of Wounds

In the shadow of pain, we rise,
With wings made of wounds, we soar high.
Each tear a testament, each scar a song,
Through trials and heartache, we find where we belong.

In the furnace of faith, our spirits ignite,
Like phoenix from ashes, we embrace the light.
Suffering transforms us, makes us anew,
With wings made of wounds, we dare to pursue.

Humbly we gather, our burdens to share,
In unity's strength, we learn how to bear.
For in brokenness, beauty is found,
With wings made of wounds, redemption profound.

Towards heights of grace, we stretch and we gleam,
In every affliction, lies God's holy dream.
Though trials may shatter, our spirits won't bend,
With wings made of wounds, our journey won't end.

O, let us not falter, no matter the storm,
Together in faith, each heart shall transform.
For we are the echoes of love that won't cease,
With wings made of wounds, our souls find their peace.

The Lament of the Lost

In shadows we wander, in silence we weep,
The lament of the lost, in memories deep.
A whisper of hope flutters like a dove,
Yet the weight of despair blots out the love.

Through alleys of anguish, we tread with care,
Each step a reminder of burdens we bear.
Nostalgia clings tightly, a bittersweet chain,
The lament of the lost sings sweetly of pain.

In twilight's embrace, we search for the light,
With eyes ever searching, we long for the sight.
But shadows persist, as echoes of grief,
The lament of the lost, a cry for relief.

Yet in every sorrow, a story unfolds,
In the heart of the broken, the truth shall be told.
For through tears and trials, we find our own worth,
The lament of the lost gives birth to new birth.

So gather we must, though the path may seem drear,
For together we rise, wiping away every tear.
In the symphony of souls, we find our own song,
The lament of the lost cannot lead us wrong.

Songs of Suffering Saints

In the stillness of night, their voices arise,
Songs of suffering saints, a heavenly guise.
With every lament, a prayer takes its flight,
Illuminating darkness, bringing forth light.

Through trials and tribulations, their faith stood tall,
In moments of silence, they answered the call.
With hearts intertwined, they danced through the pain,
Songs of suffering saints like soft summer rain.

In valleys of shadows, they sought out the dawn,
Holding on to hope as the old ways were gone.
Their spirits ignited as love's flame thrived,
Songs of suffering saints, forever revived.

O, let their stories be woven in ours,
As grace spreads its wings, lifting us like stars.
For in every heartbeat, their legacy sings,
Songs of suffering saints bring forth holy things.

So with voices united, we echo their praise,
For through pain and struggle, we find our own ways.
In the tapestry of lives, let truth always reign,
Songs of suffering saints shall never be in vain.

Refuge in the Ruins

In ruins we gather, hearts full of grace,
Finding refuge in shadows, a sacred space.
Amongst broken pillars, our spirits entwine,
In the depths of despair, the light will align.

Beneath crumbling arches, we breathe in the air,
Each sigh a reminder that love's always there.
For amid the wreckage, hope starts to bloom,
Finding refuge in ruins, we banish the gloom.

Like flowers that blossom from cracks in the stone,
We nurture our sorrows, and soon we have grown.
With hands intertwined, we craft our own fate,
Finding refuge in ruins, where grace can create.

In the quiet of night, when shadows retreat,
We gather our stories, no longer discreet.
For in every hardship, there's courage to find,
Finding refuge in ruins, our spirits unwind.

So together we stand, though the world may be torn,
In the heart of the broken, new life shall be born.
With love as our anchor, and faith as our wings,
Finding refuge in ruins, our heart's song still sings.

Celestial Music in the Chaos

In the storm where silence breaks,
A whisper calls from realms above.
Heaven's voice in tumult shakes,
Resounding chords of boundless love.

Stars align in cosmic hymn,
Painting skies with colors bright.
Amidst the dark, hope never dims,
For every shadow, there is light.

Harmony in every strife,
When chaos reigns, tune in your heart.
Each note weaves the threads of life,
A symphony where peace can start.

Angels gather, songs unfold,
In the heart of raging night.
Their melodies, a tale retold,
Lead lost souls to eternal light.

Listen close, the world may roar,
Yet divine echoes softly play.
Find the music at your core,
And let it guide you on your way.

The Dance of the Damned

In shadows deep where spirits weep,
A dance unfolds in realms unseen.
Twisting forms, both lost and steep,
They spiral in their mournful sheen.

Whispers haunt the midnight air,
Each step a tale of pain and woe.
Yet in the dark, there's strength to bear,
For even the damned can learn to grow.

With heavy hearts, they move with grace,
In every ache, a lesson learned.
And to the tempo, they embrace,
The fire in their souls still burned.

Beneath the veil of sorrow's clutch,
Resilience blooms in twilight's flow.
With every turn, they find the touch,
Of grace that leads them to let go.

In this dance, a chance to rise,
For darkness will not hold you fast.
Embrace the fear, unveil the guise,
And find the light within the past.

Blessings in the Struggle

Beneath the weight of earthly trials,
Seeds of hope begin to sprout.
With every tear, a new path smiles,
In valleys deep, we learn about.

Embrace the storm, for it will teach,
That strength lies hidden deep within.
Each setback brings a lesson rich,
A chance for growth, a chance to win.

In every heartache, grace flows free,
A gentle hand that lifts us high.
For in the struggle, we will see,
The love that never says goodbye.

Stand firm in faith when shadows loom,
For blessings rise from burdens borne.
In every dark, there's light to bloom,
A dawn awaits, a world reborn.

Through aching nights, let laughter ring,
For joy still dances in the pain.
In every loss, new hope can spring,
And love will always rise again.

A Light Beneath the Shadows

When darkness drapes the silent night,
A flicker calls from deep within.
The soul ignites, defying fright,
In whispered prayers, we rise again.

Stars that shimmer, echoes of grace,
Remind us life is more than pain.
In every heart, there's a sacred space,
Where love will always break the chain.

Underneath the weight we bear,
Hope's ember glows, just out of sight.
Through every trial, know you're rare,
A shining spark, a beacon bright.

In each moment, strength resides,
As shadows dance, do not retreat.
Embrace the change that hope provides,
And let your light spread through the street.

With every breath, let courage heal,
For in the dark, we find our shine.
A brighter world, our hearts will feel,
As love guides us, divine design.

Hymns from the Wounded Heart

In shadows deep, we find our grace,
The wounded soul seeks a warm embrace.
With every tear, a prayer we send,
To heal the heart, our spirits mend.

In silence, whispered faith will rise,
A melody beneath the skies.
Through shattered dreams, we stand in light,
United in love, we face the night.

For every scar a story told,
Of battles fought and hearts so bold.
In brokenness, we find our part,
The sacred hymn of the wounded heart.

So let us sing, in joy and pain,
In every loss, we seek to gain.
For in our hearts, a flame will spark,
A hymn of hope, from the wounded dark.

With each new dawn, our spirits soar,
In gratitude, we love once more.
Transcending grief, we find our way,
In wounded hearts, we choose to stay.

Blessings in the Ashes

From ashes rise, the spirit strong,
In every end, we find our song.
The trials faced, transformed in grace,
Blessings bloom in a sacred space.

Each scar we bear, a mark of light,
Illuminates the darkest night.
In whispers soft, the soul will know,
From deepest pain, true love will grow.

Through fire's wrath, we learn to stand,
The broken earth, a promise planned.
In every heart, a seed shall swell,
In ashes deep, our stories tell.

With open arms, we greet the dawn,
For in the dark, new hope is drawn.
Blessings found amid the strife,
Renewed in love, we claim our life.

From ashes rise, each soul a light,
In unity, our spirits bright.
For every fall, we rise once more,
Embracing love that we restore.

Prayers Uttered in Anguish

In deepest anguish, hearts cry out,
A fervent plea, a quiet shout.
Each tear a prayer, a sacred plea,
In dolor's grip, we seek to see.

Through valleys low and shadows cast,
We find in prayer, the strength to last.
A journey fraught with doubt and fear,
Yet in the pain, our faith draws near.

With gentle hands, we reach for grace,
In prayerful whispers, we find our place.
For though the night may hold us tight,
Our anguished prayers will seek the light.

In every breath, a plea for peace,
In prayers uttered, our burdens cease.
With open hearts, we yield the fight,
And find in darkness, the promise bright.

So let us pray, in hope we stand,
With anguished hearts, yet love so grand.
For every prayer, though steeped in pain,
Will lead us home, our souls' refrain.

Transcending the Trials

Amidst the trials, we shall rise,
With steadfast hearts, our spirits wise.
For every storm that shakes our ground,
In faith and love, we shall be found.

Through every tear, resilience grows,
In darkest times, true courage shows.
With open arms, we greet the fight,
Transcending trials into the light.

In unity, our voices blend,
A chorus strong that will not end.
Through struggles faced, we learn to fly,
With wings of hope, our souls defy.

For every wound, a strength we gain,
In battling pain, we break the chain.
With hearts aflame, we forge ahead,
Transcending trials, where angels tread.

So let us climb, with spirits bold,
Embracing life, as it unfolds.
In every test, a chance to see,
The beauty born from adversity.

Prayers in the Night

In silence deep, my heart does call,
To heavens bright, where angels fall.
A whispered plea, a gentle sigh,
Embraced in faith, I reach on high.

With every star, a sacred light,
Guides my soul through deepening night.
I seek the peace that knows no end,
In prayerful thoughts, my spirit mend.

The moon bears witness to my search,
In sacred whispers, I do lurch.
Each tear a token, each breath a song,
On paths of hope, where I belong.

The world may fade, but love remains,
In distant realms where grace sustains.
I lay my burdens at Your feet,
In quiet moments, my heart's retreat.

Through night's embrace, my trust will grow,
For in the dark, Your light will show.
With every word, my soul may rise,
To meet the dawn in endless skies.

The Canvas of Life's Strife

Upon the canvas, colors bleed,
A tapestry of every need.
Through trials faced and shadows cast,
We paint our tales from first to last.

With each brushstroke, pain takes flight,
A glimpse of hope, a spark of light.
In every tear, a lesson drawn,
Life's art unfolds from dusk to dawn.

The hues of grace amidst the gray,
Guide weary hearts along the way.
In faith we find our heart's true voice,
From depths of sorrow, we rejoice.

Each moment fleeting, yet divine,
In struggle fierce, Your love will shine.
We weave our stories, brush by brush,
In sacred trust, our spirits hush.

On this canvas, life does breathe,
In every fold, Your light we weave.
Through storms we learn, in peace we stand,
Life's art unfolds by Your own hand.

Spirits Rising from Ashes

From smoldered dreams, the embers glow,
Awakening souls from depths below.
In whispered flames, a truth ignites,
Resilience found in darkest nights.

Like phoenix bold, we rise anew,
In trials faced, our strength shines through.
With every scar, we've learned to fly,
Through ashes gray, we touch the sky.

Where shadows linger, hope appears,
In courage born from all our fears.
Each heart aflame, a light so bright,
Transcending darkness, we seek the light.

Through suffering's path, our spirits soar,
For love endures, and opens doors.
United in faith, we stand with grace,
From ashes risen, we find our place.

In every breath, there's life anew,
Together we rise, in all we do.
Emboldened souls will never fall,
From ashes now, we rise for all.

The Thorns of Existence

In gardens rife, where thorns do grow,
We tread with care, through pain we show.
These prickly paths of trials found,
In every wound, a love profound.

With every step, the heart does ache,
Yet through the thorns, our souls awake.
For in the shadow, light still gleams,
We find our peace in silent dreams.

The thorns remind of life's embrace,
A paradox of hope and grace.
In every struggle, strength we find,
The beauty born, of heart and mind.

Amidst the brambles, seeds are sown,
In pain and love, we have grown.
With faith as guide, we press ahead,
Through thorny trails, our spirits led.

Embracing both the joy and strife,
We cultivate the gift of life.
With every thorn, we rise and sing,
In truth, there's beauty in everything.

Milton Keynes UK
Ingram Content Group UK Ltd.
UKHW020039271124
451585UK00012B/949